SOUNDS LIKE READING™

BOOK FOUR

The Frail Snail on the Trail

A LONG VOWEL SOUNDS BOOK WITH CONSONANT BLENDS

Brian P. Cleary

illustrations by
Jason Miskimins

Consultant:
Alice M. Maday
Ph.D. in Early Childhood Education with a Focus in Literacy
Assistant Professor, Retired
Department of Curriculum and Instruction
University of Minnesota

M Millbrook Press/Minneapolis

to Mrs. Clarke,
my third-grade teacher in Richfield, Minnesota
—B.P.C.

Millbrook Press
A division of Lerner Publishing Group, Inc.
241 First Avenue North
Minneapolis, MN 55401 U.S.A.

Website address: www.lernerbooks.com

Library of Congress Cataloging-in-Publication Data

Cleary, Brian P., 1959–
    The frail snail on the trail : a long vowel sounds book with consonant blends /
by Brian P. Cleary ; illustrations by Jason Miskimins ; consultant: Alice M. Maday.
        p.   cm. — (Sounds like reading)
    ISBN 978–0–8225–7638–9 (lib. bdg. : alk. paper)
    1. English language—Vowels—Juvenile literature. 2. English language—
Consonants—Juvenile literature. 3. English language—Phonetics—Juvenile
literature. 4. Reading—Phonetic method—Juvenile literature. I. Miskimins,
Jason, ill. II. Maday, Alice M. III. Title.
PE1157.C545 2009
428.1'3—dc22   2008012773

Manufactured in the United States of America
1 2 3 4 5 6 – BP – 14 13 12 11 10 09

Dear Parents and Educators,

As a former adult literacy coach and the father of three children, I know that learning to read isn't always easy. That's why I developed **Sounds Like Reading**™—a series that uses a combination of devices to help children learn to read.

This book is the fourth in the **Sounds Like Reading**™ series. It uses rhyme, repetition, illustration, and phonics to introduce young readers to long vowel sounds and consonant blends— "sound-outable" letter combinations such as *fl*, *tr*, *br*, and *st*.

Starting on page 4, you'll see three rhyming words on each left-hand page. These words are part of the sentence on the facing page. They all feature long vowels and consonant blends. As the book progresses, the sentences become more challenging. These sentences contain a "discovery" word—an extra rhyming word in addition to those that appear on the left. Toward the end of the book, the sentences contain two discovery words. Children will delight in the increased confidence that finding and decoding these words will bring. They'll also enjoy looking for the mouse that appears throughout the book. The mouse asks readers to look for words that sound alike.

The bridge to literacy is one of the most important we will ever cross. It is my hope that the **Sounds Like Reading**™ series will help young readers to hop, gallop, and skip from one side to the other!

Sincerely,

Brian P. Cleary

Look for me to help you find the words that sound alike!

swine

twine

spine

Can you find three words that sound alike?

4

The **swine** put **twine** on my **spine**.

smoke

croak

spoke

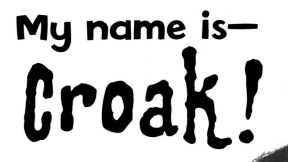

My name is—
Croak!

Can you find three words that sound alike?

The **smoke** made her **croak** as she **spoke**.

creep

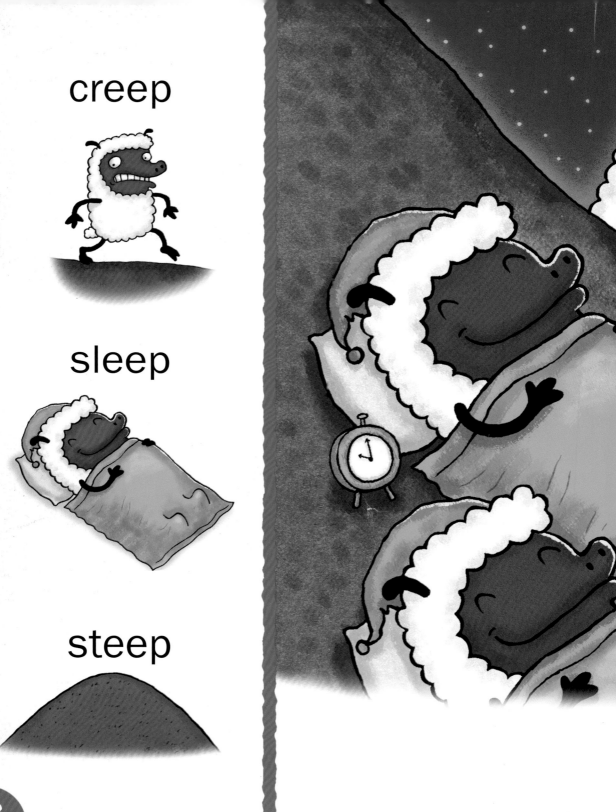

sleep

steep

Can you find three words that sound alike?

We **creep** and **sleep** on a hill that is **steep**.

frail

snail

trail

The **frail snail** is on the **trail**.

steam

cream

dream

Can you find three words that sound alike?

The **steam** came from the **cream** in a **dream**.

cry

fly

sky

Can you find the word that sounds like cry, fly, and sky?

I **cry** when I **try** to **fly** in the **sky**.

fleet

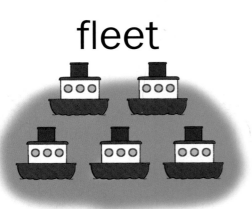

greet

sleet

Can you find the word that sounds like fleet, greet, and sleet?

The **fleet** can **meet** and **greet** in the **sleet**.

bride

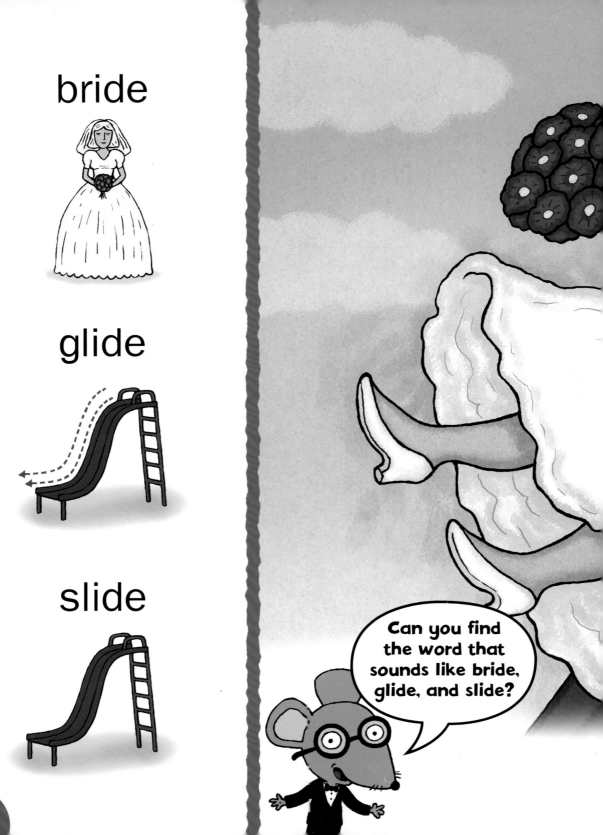

glide

slide

18

The **bride tried** to **glide** down
the **slide**.

drew

blue

glue

It is **true** that he **drew** with
blue glue.

tree

free

flee

Can you find the word that sounds like tree, free, and flee?

22

The **bee** by the **tree** was **free** to **flee**.

Blake

snake

steak

Can you find the word that sounds like Blake, snake, and steak?

24

Blake and the **snake** ate
a **steak** by the **lake**.

price

spice

slice

Can you find two words that sound like price, spice, and slice?

The **mice** paid **twice** the **price** for the **spice** and the **slice**.

grain

GRAIN

Spain

S P A I N

drain

Can you find two words that sound like grain, Spain, and drain?

The **plain grain** from **Spain** fell into the **main drain**.

flew

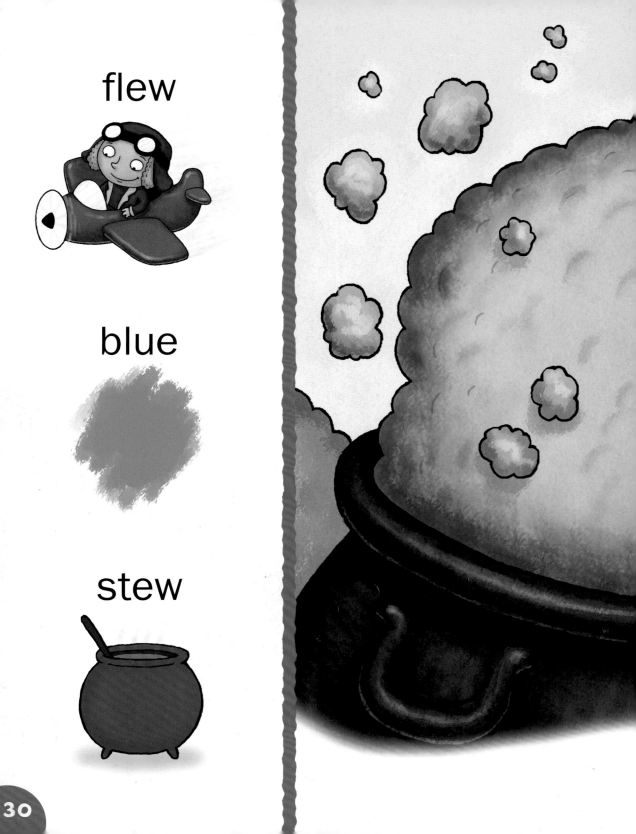

blue

stew

Can you find two words that sound like flew, blue, and stew?

Sue flew as the **blue stew grew**.

Brian P. Cleary is the author of the best-selling Words Are CATegorical® series as well as the Math Is CATegorical® and Adventures in Memory™ series. He has also written several picture books and poetry books. In addition to his work as a children's author and humorist, Mr. Cleary has been a tutor in an adult literacy program. He lives in Cleveland, Ohio.

Jason Miskimins grew up in Cincinnati, Ohio, and graduated from the Columbus College of Art & Design in 2003. He currently lives in North Olmsted, Ohio, where he works as an illustrator of books and greeting cards.

Alice M. Maday has a master's degree in early childhood education from Butler University in Indianapolis, Indiana, and a Ph.D. in early childhood education, with a focus in literacy, from the University of Minnesota in Minneapolis. Dr. Maday has taught at the college level as well as in elementary schools and preschools throughout the country. In addition, she has served as an emergent literacy educator for kindergarten and first-grade students in Germany for the U.S. Department of Defense. Her research interests include the kindergarten curriculum, emergent literacy, parent and teacher expectations, and the place of preschool in the reading readiness process.

For even more phonics fun, check out all eight SOUNDS LIKE READING™ titles listed on the back of this book!

And find activities, games, and more at www.brianpcleary.com.